Contents

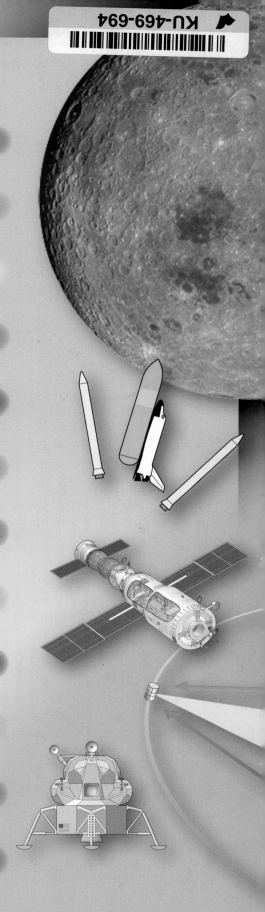

Weblink: www.CurriculumVisions.com/space

Rockets

Gravity is a force that pulls everything towards the Earth. So if you want to get into space you have to push hard against it.

Why is it so difficult to get into SPACE? The reason is that everything is pulled towards the Earth by an invisible force. This force is called GRAVITY. To get into space, you have to overcome the force of gravity.

Fireworks

A firework shows you how hard it is. Almost the whole inside of the firework has to be packed with fuel. The part that explodes, or sends out a shower of lights – called the PAYLOAD – is in the nose cone.

How rockets work

ROCKETS have to lift the fuel and the payload (for example, a spaceship or SATELLITE) (pictures ① and ③). So, the more the payload weighs, the more fuel is going to be needed to get it into space.

It would be simple to launch a payload using a rocket filled with solid fuel – just like a giant firework. But you can't control this kind of rocket. For that you have to use gases, which is more like the way a motor car works (picture ②).

▶ ① **When a rocket fires it sends out gases downwards so fast that the rocket is pushed up.**

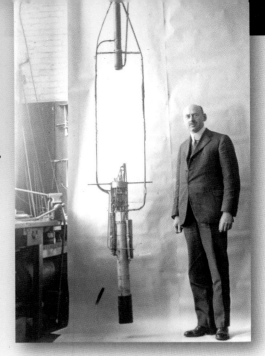

▲ ② **Robert Goddard was a rocket pioneer. In 1925, when this picture was taken, he was already using two different liquids as a fuel, which were mixed in a pump and then burned to make gas. Notice that everything was made on an engineer's workbench – very different from making rockets today.**

In a motor car you turn petrol into fine droplets and mix it with oxygen in the air, then burn the mixture. Burning the mixture causes air to expand in the cylinders and that pushes the wheels around.

In space there is no air, so the oxygen has to be carried. It is cooled and carried as liquid oxygen. Petrol would not give enough power, so another fuel is used – often liquid hydrogen gas. The power is controlled by the rate the gases are pumped to the engine.

The rocket is steered by tilting the engines.

Journey
ace

Glossary

ATMOSPHERE

The envelope of gases that surrounds the Earth and other bodies in the universe.

AXIS (pl. **AXES**)

The line around which a body spins. The Earth spins around an axis through its north and south geographic poles.

CAPSULE

A small pressurised space vehicle.

DOCK

To meet with and attach to another space vehicle.

DRAG

A force that hinders the movement of something.

FRICTION

The force that resists two bodies that are in contact.

GEOSTATIONARY SATELLITE

An artificial satellite in a fixed or geosynchronous orbit around the Earth.

GRAVITY

The force of attraction between bodies. The larger an object, the more its gravitational pull on other objects. The Sun's gravity is the most powerful in the Solar System, keeping all of the planets and other materials within the Solar System.

HEAT SHIELD

A protective device on the outside of a space vehicle that absorbs the heat during re-entry, and protects it from burning up.

LAUNCH VEHICLE/ LAUNCHER

A system of propellant tanks and rocket motors or engines designed to lift a payload into space. It may, or may not, be part of a space vehicle.

LIGHT-YEAR

The distance travelled by light through space in one Earth year.

MODULE

A section, or part, of a space vehicle.

PAYLOAD

The spacecraft that is carried into space by a launcher.

PROBE

An unmanned spacecraft designed to explore our Solar System and beyond. Voyager, Cassini, and Magellan are examples of probes.

ROCKET

Any kind of device that uses the principle of jet propulsion, that is, the rapid release of gases designed to propel an object rapidly.

SATELLITE

An artificial object that orbits the Earth. Usually used as a term for an unmanned spacecraft whose job is to acquire or transfer data to and from the ground.

SLINGSHOT TRAJECTORY

A path chosen to use the attractive force of gravity to increase the speed of a spacecraft. The craft is flown toward the planet or star, and it speeds up under the gravitational force. At the correct moment the path is taken to send the spacecraft into orbit and, when pointing in the right direction, to turn it from orbit, with its increased velocity, toward the final destination.

SONIC BOOM

The noise created when an object moves faster than the speed of sound.

SPACE

Everything beyond the Earth's atmosphere.

The word "space" is used rather generally. It can be divided up into inner space – the Solar System, and outer space – everything beyond the Solar System.

SPACE STATION

A large artificial satellite used as a base for operations in space.

STAR

A large ball of gases that radiates light. The star nearest the Earth is the Sun. There are enormous numbers of stars in the universe, but few can be seen with the naked eye. Stars may occur singly, as our Sun, or in groups, of which pairs are most common.

TRAJECTORY

The curved path followed by a projectile.

VACUUM

A space which does not contain any matter. Outer space is a vacuum.

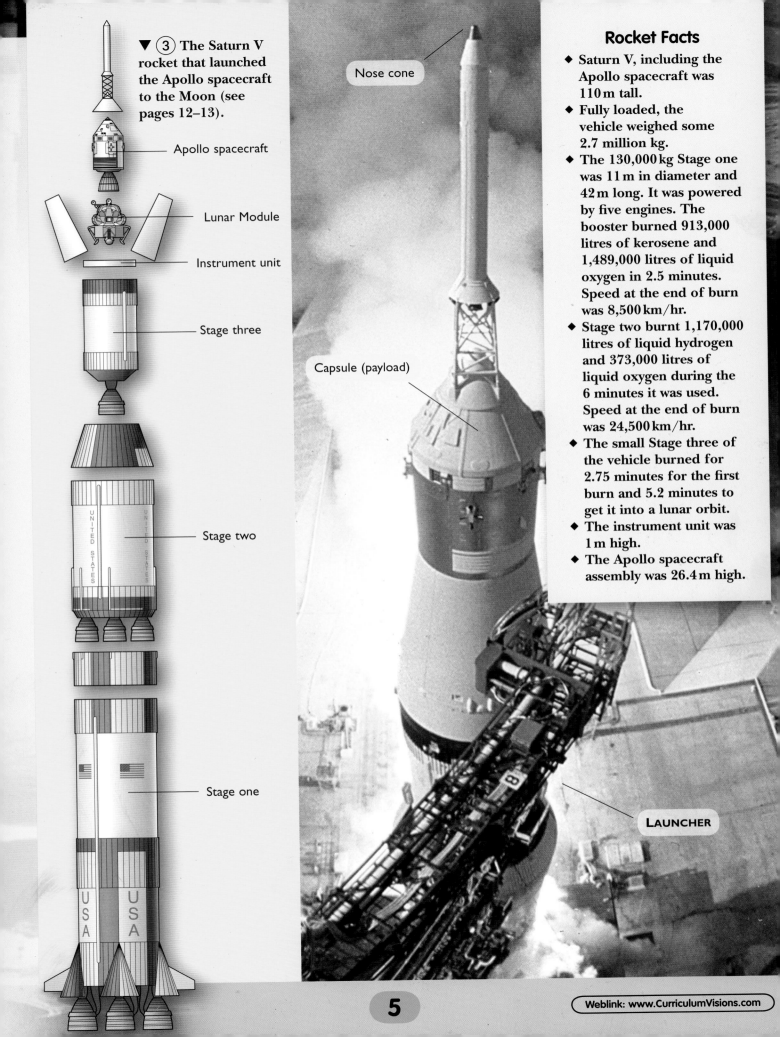

▼ ③ The Saturn V rocket that launched the Apollo spacecraft to the Moon (see pages 12–13).

Apollo spacecraft

Lunar Module

Instrument unit

Stage three

Stage two

UNITED STATES

Stage one

USA

Nose cone

Capsule (payload)

LAUNCHER

Rocket Facts

◆ Saturn V, including the Apollo spacecraft was 110 m tall.

◆ Fully loaded, the vehicle weighed some 2.7 million kg.

◆ The 130,000 kg Stage one was 11 m in diameter and 42 m long. It was powered by five engines. The booster burned 913,000 litres of kerosene and 1,489,000 litres of liquid oxygen in 2.5 minutes. Speed at the end of burn was 8,500 km/hr.

◆ Stage two burnt 1,170,000 litres of liquid hydrogen and 373,000 litres of liquid oxygen during the 6 minutes it was used. Speed at the end of burn was 24,500 km/hr.

◆ The small Stage three of the vehicle burned for 2.75 minutes for the first burn and 5.2 minutes to get it into a lunar orbit.

◆ The instrument unit was 1 m high.

◆ The Apollo spacecraft assembly was 26.4 m high.

Satellites

Most spacecraft are satellites. They are small objects that circle the Earth.

When we think of a journey into space, we may imagine spacecraft going to distant places. But these are expensive and rare events. Most spacecraft are humble boxes of electronics, circling above us in space. These are called SATELLITES (picture ③).

What satellites do

The first satellite was the Russian Sputnik (picture ①). It was a tremendous breakthrough in science. People across the world could hear its warbling sounds over the radio.

In space there are now thousands of satellites looking down on us, or sending messages from one part of the world to another. We take them for granted, but they are a vital part of our world.

There are two kinds of satellite. One kind is placed just over 35,786 km above the Earth's surface. In this position it circles the Earth at the same rate as the Earth spins on its AXIS. As a result it seems to be stationary. We call these GEOSTATIONARY SATELLITES. They are mainly used for sending messages by telephone, radio or television. Just three satellites spaced evenly at the equator can send messages across the world (picture ②). Some weather satellites and spy satellites are also placed over the equator.

▲ ① Sputnik, the Russian for traveller, was launched on October 4, 1957. This was the first human-made object in space. It was a hollow metal ball with a radio transmitter, four aerials and a simple way of measuring temperature.

Sputnik was powered by internal batteries and its signal stopped when the batteries ran out 21 days after launch.

The launch of Sputnik 1 was followed a month later by Sputnik 2, which carried a live dog, named Laika, the first living thing in space.

The other kind of satellite is placed in orbit closer to the Earth. It no longer keeps pace with the Earth's spin, but sweeps across the Earth's surface. These satellites can look down on details of the Earth, and they are used for such things as mapping the Earth's surface, weather forecasting – and spying.

▼ ② This diagram shows how three satellites placed 35,786 km above the Earth can send signals across the world. A ground station sends a signal to its nearest satellite. This relays the message to the satellite and then a ground receiver picks up the relayed message. In this way, a television signal sent from Sydney, Australia, for example, can reach London, England, almost instantaneously.

Satellite Facts

◆ Satellites can be placed in different orbits. Satellites that travel from pole to pole are in a low orbit of about 1,000 km. Some weather satellites are of this kind. Global position satellites are placed about 20,000 km above the surface.

◆ Any satellite placed 35,786 km above the surface of the Earth will travel at the same speed as the Earth and will appear stationary. This orbit is used for communications satellites, such as those sending telephone and television signals.

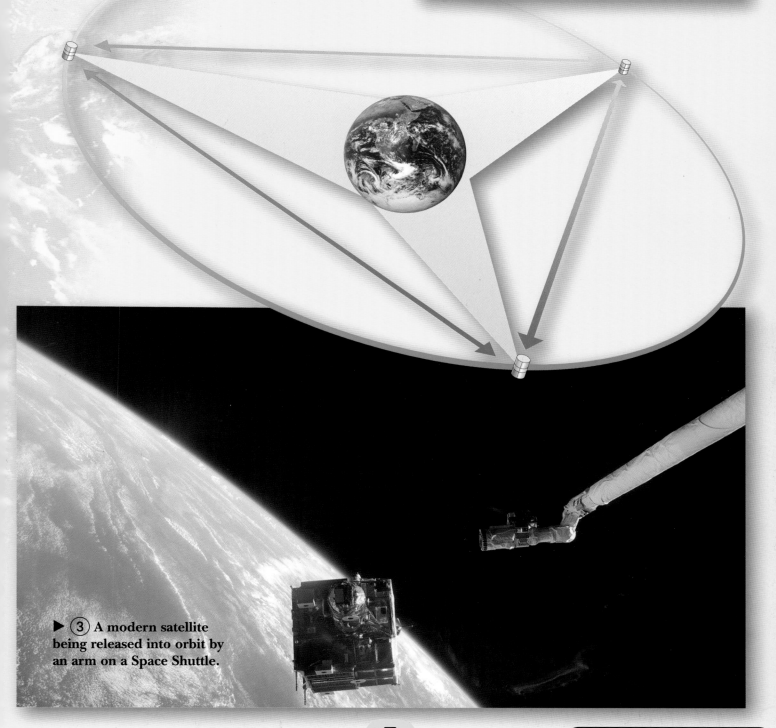

▶ ③ A modern satellite being released into orbit by an arm on a Space Shuttle.

7

Survival in space

Satellites are easy to get into space. But getting people into space is a much bigger challenge. Now we plan to go to Mars, but how will people survive such long journeys?

We live on a planet that is surrounded by life-giving oxygen. We are firmly anchored to the surface by **GRAVITY**, over three quarters of the planet is water and the soil is fertile so plants will grow in it and provide our food. In space there are none of these things. We must take what we need with us and find ways of doing without what we cannot take.

▼ ① When astronauts work outside of their spacecraft they need complete life support systems, such as pressure suits and backpacks (which contain cooling fluid, oxygen, toilet facilities, power source and communications equipment).

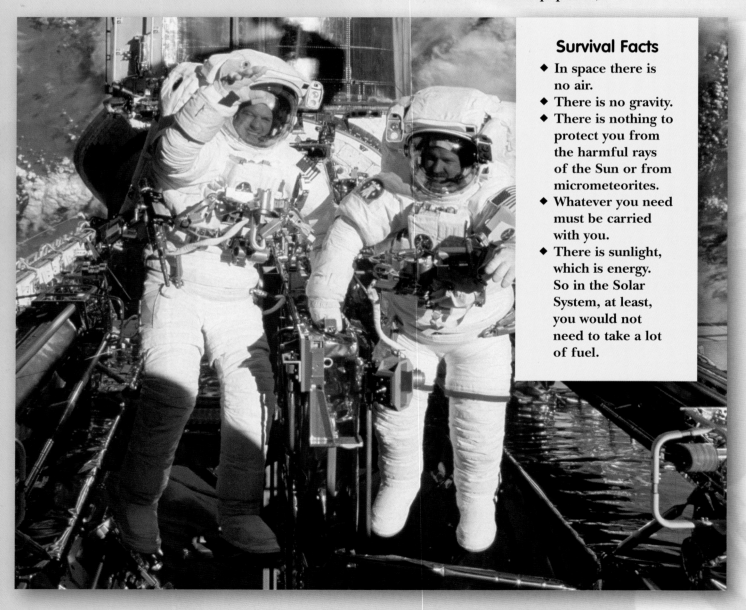

Survival Facts

◆ In space there is no air.
◆ There is no gravity.
◆ There is nothing to protect you from the harmful rays of the Sun or from micrometeorites.
◆ Whatever you need must be carried with you.
◆ There is sunlight, which is energy. So in the Solar System, at least, you would not need to take a lot of fuel.

Living in a vacuum

There is no air in space. It is a VACUUM. If we live inside a spacecraft or in a spacesuit, we must fill it with air to give the same pressure as on Earth. We must also build spacesuits (picture ①) and spacecraft strong enough so they will not burst apart from the air pressure on the inside and a vacuum on the outside.

Living without gravity

Gravity, the force that anchors us on the Earth's surface, works because of the huge size of the Earth. We cannot imitate it in any way. Our bodies live with gravity, and their size and shape depend on it. When we go to places without gravity, our bodies have no force pulling on them and so, in time, they change shape.

▼ ② In a weightless environment foods and liquids simply float about. Most drink has to be sucked through a tube and even food can be hard to catch unless it is inside a container.

Living without air

Our air contains the oxygen we need to live. On Earth, the air is cleaned and renewed, thanks to plants. In space, a supply of air has to be taken along, and the carbon dioxide that we breathe out has to be removed.

Living without water

On Earth, water is abundant. There is none in space. We are used to cleaning and purifying our water, however, so reusing our supply of water would not be a major problem.

Living without food

There is no way that food can be found in space and it must all be taken with us (picture ②). Food is mostly water and so it can be dried and made smaller. But it cannot be recycled. What we need has to be taken, and on a long journey this could be a very bulky item.

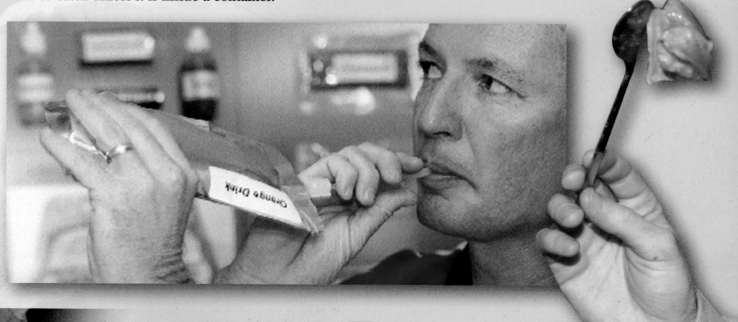

The first manned spacecraft

The first manned spacecraft were just big enough for one person. But the problems of safe takeoff and return to Earth were still immense.

The difference between launching a satellite and a manned spacecraft is huge. The satellite does not need to breathe, eat or drink. It is small and, at the end of its life, it can just be allowed to burn up as it plunges back to Earth.

When you need to plan for carrying people, you have to plan for their safety, including bringing them back to the Earth safe and well.

Takeoff

The first problem is takeoff. As **ROCKETS** leave the ground, the people inside the spacecraft experience a great **DRAG** from **GRAVITY**. It can be as much as 6 **G** (six times the Earth's gravity). If the spacecraft takes off too fast, this drag could kill the astronauts. As a result, manned spacecraft have to take off much more slowly than rockets launching satellites.

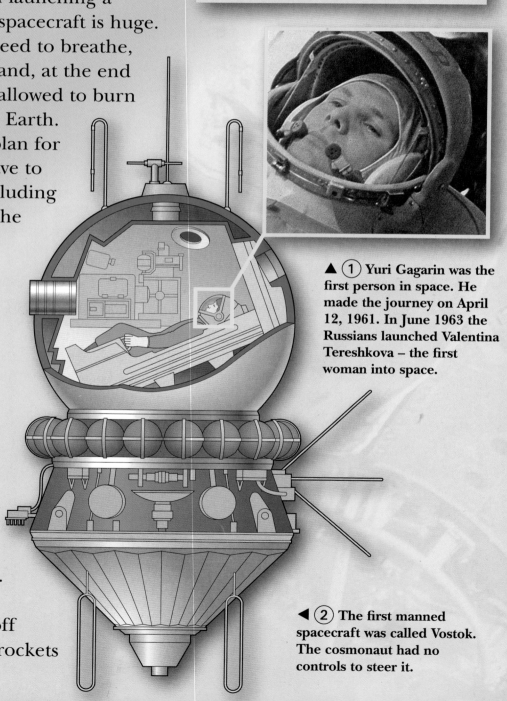

▲ ① Yuri Gagarin was the first person in space. He made the journey on April 12, 1961. In June 1963 the Russians launched Valentina Tereshkova – the first woman into space.

◄ ② The first manned spacecraft was called Vostok. The cosmonaut had no controls to steer it.

▼ ③ The Redstone rocket used to make the first American space journey.

◄ ④ Alan B Shepard was the first American in space. He made a short journey on May 5, 1961. The first American to orbit the Earth was John Glenn (shown left) on February 20, 1962, in 'Friendship 7'.

Returning

Returning is hardest of all. A spacecraft begins its descent travelling at 25,000 km an hour. It cannot fall to the ground at this speed without smashing to pieces. So the craft has to return gradually, making closer and closer orbits while it loses speed.

The **ATMOSPHERE** is used as a natural brake. But this also causes the spacecraft to become extremely hot, and excellent **HEAT SHIELDS** are needed.

The first Russian cosmonauts did not land (pictures ① and ②). They ejected from their craft and came to Earth by parachute. The Americans landed their space **CAPSULES** in the sea to lessen the impact (pictures ③, ④ and ⑤). The modern Space Shuttle glides back to Earth and lands on a runway.

▼ ⑤ This picture shows navy divers installing a flotation collar around the American space capsule nicknamed 'Faith 7' on May 16, 1963.

Weblink: www.CurriculumVisions.com

◆ The Apollo spacecraft weighed 50 tonnes.
◆ The launching Saturn V rocket weighed 2,700 tonnes.
◆ Three people made the first Moon landing in Apollo 11: Neil Armstrong and 'Buzz' Aldrin actually walked on the Moon; Michael Collins remained in the orbiting Command Module.

◀▲ ① The Gemini spacecraft.

Journey to the Moon

The journey to the Moon was the most spectacular achievement of the 20th century.

In May 1961, President John F Kennedy announced to an astonished world that, by 1969, America would land people on the Moon. To achieve this, astronauts and scientists would have to find out how to manoeuvre a spacecraft, how to meet and **DOCK** with another spacecraft, and how to walk in space.

The Gemini programme

The programme started with a two-astronaut, bell-shaped spacecraft called Gemini (picture ①). It comprised a re-entry **CAPSULE** and a section containing the rockets needed for steering in space. There was also a simple on-board computer.

To get these spacecraft into orbit, a new **LAUNCHER** was needed. This was called Titan 2.

The Apollo project

The project to reach the Moon was called Apollo. It involved a very powerful launch vehicle called Saturn V. This was needed because the spacecraft it was to launch into a lunar **TRAJECTORY** weighed 50 tonnes.

The Apollo spacecraft was made of three parts: the control centre was called the Command Module; below it, in the Service Module, was most of the food, water and fuel supplies; on top of it was the small Lunar Module (nicknamed 'Eagle') that did the landing and then returned to the orbiting Command Module and Service Module. 'Eagle' and the Service Module were uncoupled before re-entry and only the Command Module returned to Earth (pictures ②, ③ and ④).

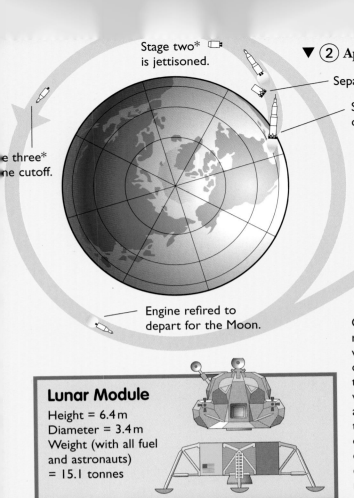

Stage two* is jettisoned.

Separation from Stage one*.

▼ (2) **Apollo Mission leaving Earth.**

Stage one* fired and liftoff of the Saturn V rocket.

Apollo separates from Stage three* and turns around to dock with Lunar Module.

...e three* ...ne cutoff.

Engine refired to depart for the Moon.

Apollo and Lunar Module approach the Moon docked together. They orbit at an average of 200 km above the surface.

▼ (3) **Apollo Mission lunar landing.**

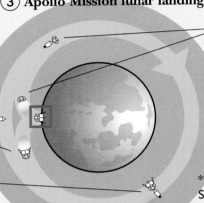

One astronaut remains in Apollo while the two others transfer to Lunar Module which separates and descends to the Moon on a lower orbit. Landing controlled with rocket engines.

After surface exploration the upper stage of the Lunar Module blasts off using the descent stage as a launch pad. It then docks with Apollo.

*see diagram page 5 for Saturn V rocket stages.

Lunar Module

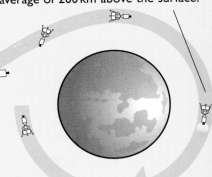

Height = 6.4 m
Diameter = 3.4 m
Weight (with all fuel and astronauts) = 15.1 tonnes

To the Moon – carefully

Nobody wanted to make such an adventure without many small, careful steps. So it was Apollo 11 that finally made a landing on the surface of the Moon on July 20, 1969.

Between this and December 1972 a total of 12 people travelled to the Moon's surface. Finally, this hugely costly, but immensely satisfying, programme was brought to a close.

▼ (4) **Apollo Mission returning home.**

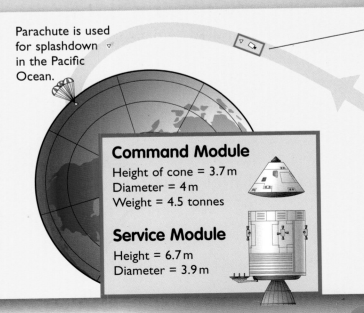

Parachute is used for splashdown in the Pacific Ocean.

As Apollo falls to Earth the service module and rockets are jettisoned, leaving the Command Module. This turns around so that the blunt end is forward.

The Moon landing astronauts transfer back to Apollo. The Lunar Module is jettisoned.

Command Module

Height of cone = 3.7 m
Diameter = 4 m
Weight = 4.5 tonnes

Service Module

Height = 6.7 m
Diameter = 3.9 m

Main engine on Apollo spacecraft is fired to escape the Moon's gravity and begins the journey back to Earth.

Weblink: www.CurriculumVisions.com

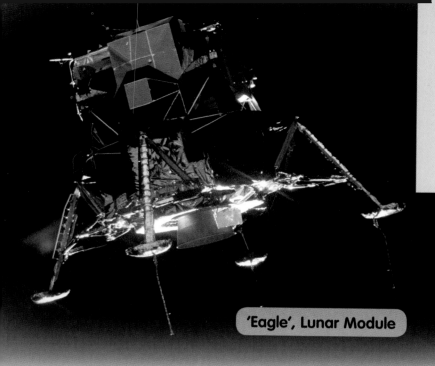

'Eagle', Lunar Module

▶ ① An astronaut's footprint on the Moon. It shows the thin, dusty 'soil'.

On the Moon

When the Lunar Module landed on the Moon, people were able to investigate a new world for the first time.

Apollo 11's Lunar Module, with two astronauts on board, finally made a lunar landing – with astronaut Neil Armstrong the first human to set foot on the Moon's surface.

Neil Armstrong stepped onto the Moon's surface at 2:56 a.m. GMT, on July 20, 1969 (pictures ① and ②).

Armstrong and 'Buzz' Aldrin remained on the Moon's surface for a day, setting up instruments and collecting samples before lifting off in 'Eagle' and returning to the Command Module. They touched down in the Pacific Ocean on July 24.

Because it was not known if there was life on the Moon, decontamination and quarantine were arranged.

Moving about

The first astronauts to land on the Moon had to stay close to the Lunar Module because they had no transport. Apollo 15, launched on July 26, 1971, carried a Moon Rover, a four-wheeled, battery-powered car that allowed the astronauts to explore greater areas of the Moon's surface (picture ③).

◀ ② Walking on the Moon was "one small step for man, one giant leap for mankind". This picture shows astronaut Neil A Armstrong, Apollo 11 mission commander, at the Lunar Module 'Eagle' on the historic first walk on the Moon's surface.

▼ ③ To get anywhere on the Moon it was necessary to have a means of transport. The Moon Rover was developed for this. It is very wide so that it is more stable on rough ground.

Weblink: www.CurriculumVisions.com

Journey to the planets

It is not possible to send people on long space journeys. But we have learned much from sending space probes.

People do not journey to other worlds; this is done by unmanned spacecraft, called **PROBES** (pictures ① and ③).

How to reach a planet

If you want to reach a distant planet, you cannot aim straight at it. Every planet is travelling fast through space. You also need to pick your time. The best time to reach a planet is when it is closest to the Earth because it takes less time and less fuel to get there.

The path needed to reach the planets has to be carefully calculated. Most probes are sent in a curve, often going close to another planet to pick up speed (a **SLINGSHOT TRAJECTORY**).

Early probes

The first probe ever to reach another planet was the American Mariner 2, in 1962. This flew past Venus. It had no cameras, but did record temperature measurements and showed conclusively that Venus was extremely hot.

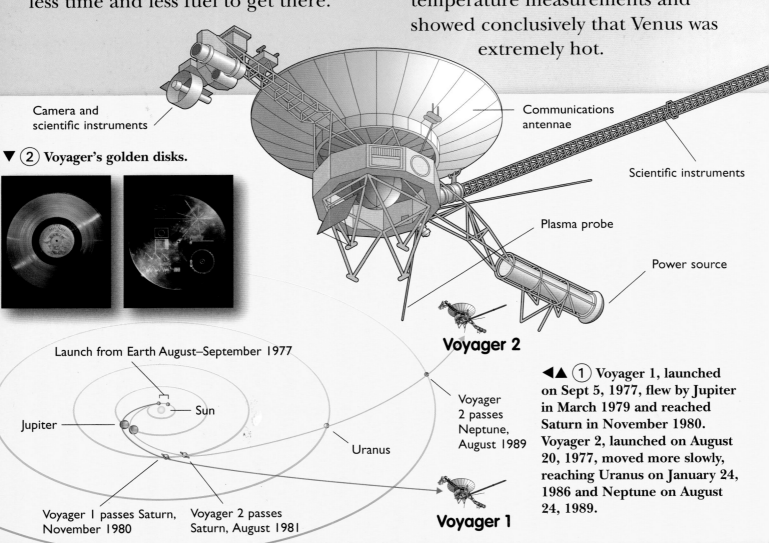

Camera and scientific instruments

▼ ② Voyager's golden disks.

Communications antennae

Scientific instruments

Plasma probe

Power source

Voyager 2

Launch from Earth August–September 1977

Sun

Jupiter

Uranus

Voyager 2 passes Neptune, August 1989

Voyager 1 passes Saturn, November 1980

Voyager 2 passes Saturn, August 1981

Voyager 1

◀▲ ① Voyager 1, launched on Sept 5, 1977, flew by Jupiter in March 1979 and reached Saturn in November 1980. Voyager 2, launched on August 20, 1977, moved more slowly, reaching Uranus on January 24, 1986 and Neptune on August 24, 1989.

▲ ③ An artist's impression of the Cassini probe approaching Saturn in 2004.

The first probes to soft land on another planet were the Russian Venera 9 and 10 in October 1975. They dropped landers on Venus and were able to send back pictures from the surface.

Voyager

The journey that caught everyone's imagination was the voyage of two identical probes called Voyager which were sent to investigate the outer planets (picture ①). They explored four planets – Jupiter, Saturn, Uranus and Neptune – as well as dozens of moons, and their rings.

The Voyagers have now left the Solar System, heading for unknown worlds. These space probes took far better pictures of the gas planets than had previously been possible. They carry golden disks telling about the Earth in case they are found by other life forms (picture ②).

These spacecraft, each weighing just under a tonne, were designed for journeys in which there would be no possibility of repair. They had to be entirely reliable and built to last the many years of the journey. The radio transmitters are able to send signals back to Earth over distances of billions of kilometres. The Voyagers have now travelled more than 14 billion km (to the edge of the Solar System).

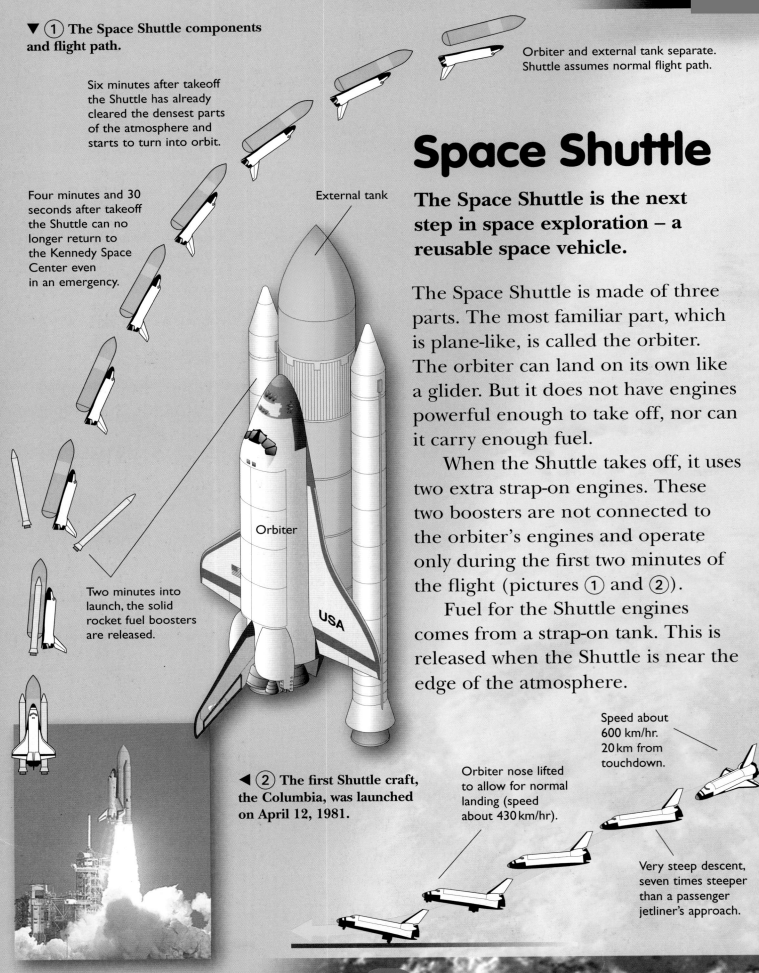

▼ ① **The Space Shuttle components and flight path.**

Orbiter and external tank separate. Shuttle assumes normal flight path.

Six minutes after takeoff the Shuttle has already cleared the densest parts of the atmosphere and starts to turn into orbit.

Four minutes and 30 seconds after takeoff the Shuttle can no longer return to the Kennedy Space Center even in an emergency.

External tank

Orbiter

Space Shuttle

The Space Shuttle is the next step in space exploration – a reusable space vehicle.

The Space Shuttle is made of three parts. The most familiar part, which is plane-like, is called the orbiter. The orbiter can land on its own like a glider. But it does not have engines powerful enough to take off, nor can it carry enough fuel.

When the Shuttle takes off, it uses two extra strap-on engines. These two boosters are not connected to the orbiter's engines and operate only during the first two minutes of the flight (pictures ① and ②).

Fuel for the Shuttle engines comes from a strap-on tank. This is released when the Shuttle is near the edge of the atmosphere.

USA

Two minutes into launch, the solid rocket fuel boosters are released.

◄ ② **The first Shuttle craft, the Columbia, was launched on April 12, 1981.**

Orbiter nose lifted to allow for normal landing (speed about 430 km/hr).

Speed about 600 km/hr. 20 km from touchdown.

Very steep descent, seven times steeper than a passenger jetliner's approach.

18

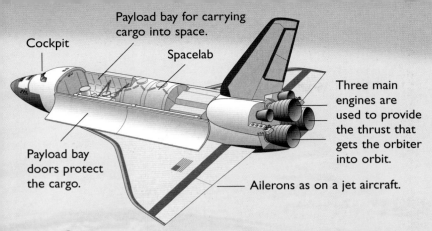

Cockpit

Payload bay for carrying cargo into space.

Spacelab

Three main engines are used to provide the thrust that gets the orbiter into orbit.

Payload bay doors protect the cargo.

Ailerons as on a jet aircraft.

▼▲ ③ The orbiter cockpit (*below*) and payload bay (*above*).

Space Shuttle Facts

◆ The Shuttle is just over 37 m long and has a wing span of just under 24 m. Fully loaded and waiting for takeoff, together with the external tank and boosters, it weighs just over 2,000 tonnes! The Shuttle is only 113 tonnes of this. All of the rest is rocket and fuel. The boosters and tank make the final length of the Shuttle at launch just over 56 m.

◆ The payload bay is over 18 m long and nearly 5 m wide. It can also carry a spacelab, and loads weighing as much as 24 tonnes, into space and 16 tonnes back to Earth.

Gliding back to Earth

The orbiter is not an aeroplane, but a glider (picture ③). The orbiter begins re-entry at about 122 km from the Earth's surface and follows a glide path 8,000 km long (picture ④).

As the orbiter sinks further and further into the atmosphere, **FRICTION** with the air acts as a natural brake.

At 40 km from the runway the orbiter is still flying at the speed of sound and so creates a **SONIC BOOM** which can be heard by people on the ground.

The orbiter lands by following a glide path which is 20 times faster and seven times steeper than an ordinary large aeroplane. It puts down its undercarriage and lands at 430 km/hr on a runway that is nearly 5 km long.

▼ ④ The way a Space Shuttle lands.

Engines fire an hour before touchdown

Surface heats up (speed about 25,000 km/hr).

Nose-up position 3,000 km from touchdown.

Very steep descent. 1,000 km from touchdown.

S turns are made to slow down the orbiter.

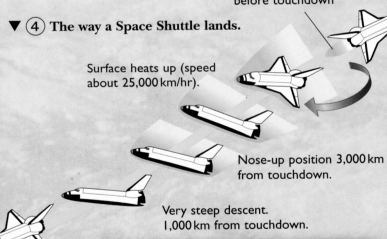

Space station

A space station is a giant step forward in getting into space. It has also been a giant step forward in international co-operation.

SPACE STATIONS may be weightless in orbit, but they are very heavy when on the ground. As a result, a whole space station cannot simply be lifted into orbit on one launch. Assembly has to happen in pieces, and the pieces – usually tubes with airlocks at both ends, and called MODULES – fitted together in space.

Early space stations

The Russians were the first to put up a space station. In 1971 they launched the 15 m long Salyut space station. They also built a ferry craft called Soyuz. It could carry three cosmonauts to and from the space station. It was, however, not reusable. It crash-landed on re-entry to Earth. They also built an unmanned ferry craft, called Progress, for transporting provisions, oxygen, water and so on.

Skylab was the first American space station. It was launched in 1973. It was made of four modules.

Mir (the Russian word for 'peace') was launched by the Russians in 1986 to replace Salyut (pictures ① and ②). Its core module weighed 23 tonnes, was 13 m long and 4.2 m wide. Eventually five more modules were added. Mir crewman, Valery Polyakov, spent a record 438 days in space.

▲ ① **Mir was a new period of co-operation between Russian cosmonauts and American astronauts. The first astronauts docked with Mir in 1995 using the Space Shuttle. Notice how large the Shuttle is compared to Mir. Each of Mir's modules could be fitted in the cargo bay of the Shuttle.**

▶ ② **The core section of Mir.**

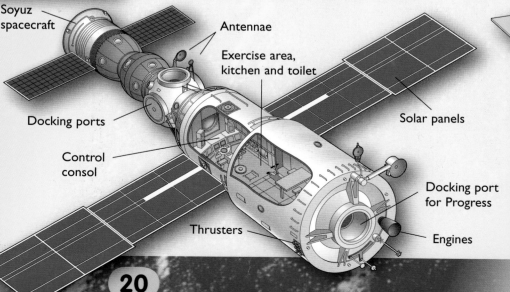

Soyuz spacecraft

Antennae

Exercise area, kitchen and toilet

Docking ports

Solar panels

Control consol

Docking port for Progress

Thrusters

Engines

▲ ③ **Looking at the International Space Station from the Space Shuttle.**

International Space Station (ISS)

The ISS is bigger by far than anything ever sent into space (pictures ③ and ④). It is also the first station to be built by many co-operating nations. It weighs 453 tonnes, is 111 m long and has a crew of six or seven living in an area the same size as a jumbo jet. It orbits 4,000 kilometres above the surface of the Earth.

▼ ④ **The main components of the International Space Station, showing which country made each component.**

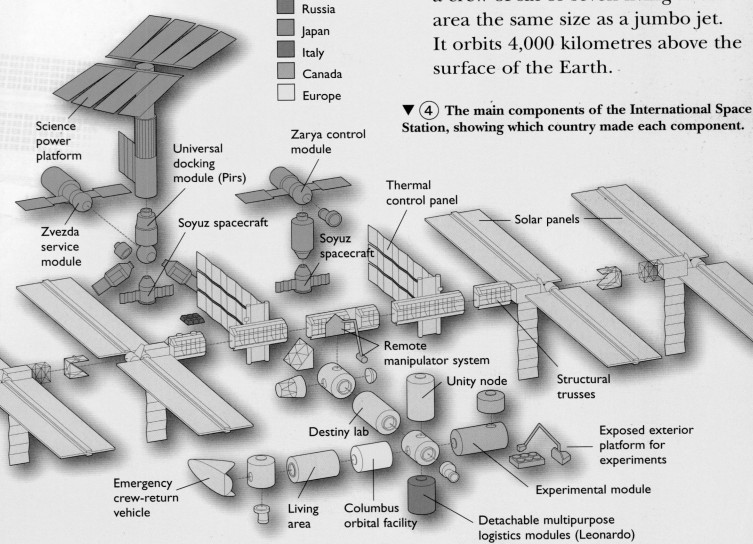

Key

- U.S.
- Russia
- Japan
- Italy
- Canada
- Europe

Science power platform

Zvezda service module

Universal docking module (Pirs)

Zarya control module

Soyuz spacecraft

Soyuz spacecraft

Thermal control panel

Solar panels

Remote manipulator system

Unity node

Structural trusses

Destiny lab

Exposed exterior platform for experiments

Experimental module

Emergency crew-return vehicle

Living area

Columbus orbital facility

Detachable multipurpose logistics modules (Leonardo)

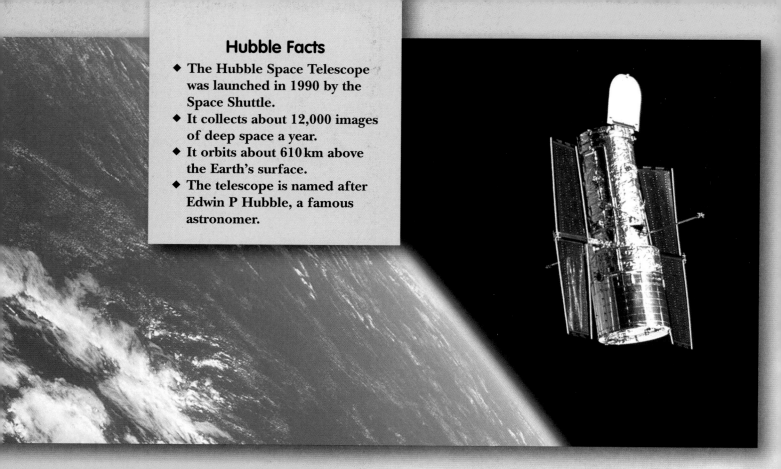

▲ ① The Hubble Space Telescope.

Looking into space

Using space telescopes we can see into space and also back in time.

Our atmosphere is made of gases and dust. They soak up and bounce back much of the light that reaches the Earth. This is why we see only the brightest **STARS** above us.

If you were able to take the dust away, the sky would immediately appear to have vastly more stars in it.

Look up again and see the stars twinkling. They do not, of course, twinkle, any more than does our Sun. The effect you see is the result of air movements. If there were no air, the stars would not twinkle and instead would become clear.

As you can see, it makes sense to try to get telescopes in orbit above the atmosphere.

Hubble Space Telescope

By far the most powerful telescope in orbit is called the Hubble Space Telescope (picture ①). It has a mirror nearly 2.5 m across. It can see objects about a billionth as faint as could be seen with the naked eye on Earth and ten times better than the most powerful telescope on Earth (pictures ② and ③).

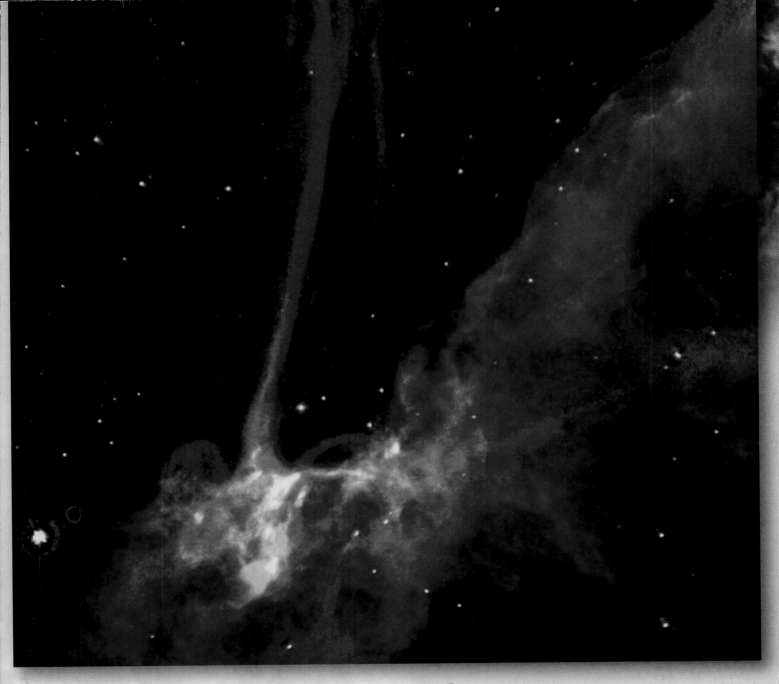

▲ ② This is an image taken by the Hubble Space Telescope. It shows gases moving outwards from a star that blew itself to pieces about 15,000 years ago. It is so far away that it has taken all this time for light from the explosion to reach us.

▼ ③ This is a galaxy 60 million LIGHT-YEARS away. The colour is produced by billions of stars.

Other astronomical satellites

Hubble is not alone. There are satellites looking at the Sun, and others designed to look for faint traces of what the universe was like when it was much younger.

Index

Curriculum Visions is a registered trademark of Atlantic Europe Publishing Company Ltd.

◆ *Atlantic Europe Publishing*

First published in 2004 by
Atlantic Europe Publishing Company Ltd

Copyright © 2004
Atlantic Europe Publishing Company Ltd

All rights reserved. No part of this publication may be reproduced, stored in a retrieval system, or transmitted in any form or by any means, electronic, mechanical, photocopying, recording or otherwise, without prior permission of the publisher.

Author
Brian Knapp, BSc, PhD
Art Director
Duncan McCrae, BSc
Senior Designer
Adele Humphries, BA, PGCE
Editors
Lisa Magloff, MA, and Gillian Gatehouse
Illustrations on behalf of
Earthscape Editions
David Woodroffe
Designed and produced by
EARTHSCAPE EDITIONS
Printed in China by
WKT Company Ltd.

Journey into space – *Curriculum Visions*
A CIP record for this book is available from the British Library.

Paperback ISBN 1 86214 392 7
Hardback ISBN 1 86214 393 5

Picture credits
All photographs courtesy of NASA, except the following: (c=centre t=top b=bottom l=left r=right) *Earthscape Editions* 3, 4b, 5l, 7t, 10b, 12tc, 13, 16c, 16bl, 18tl, 18–19b, 19tl, 20b, 21b.

This product is manufactured from sustainable managed forests. For every tree cut down at least one more is planted.

The Curriculum Visions web site
Details of our other products can be found at:

www.CurriculumVisions.com